D0594348

For Grandma

Compiled by
Christina Anello

 PETER PAUPER PRESS, INC.
WHITE PLAINS, NEW YORK

Text border by
Jo Gershman

For my loving Grandmas—
Anna and Antoinette

Copyright © 1992
Peter Pauper Press, Inc.
202 Mamaroneck Avenue
White Plains, NY 10601
ISBN 0-88088-754-0
Printed in China
15 14 13 12 11 10

FOR GRANDMA

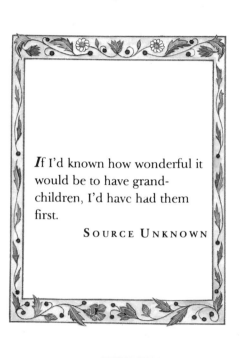

If I'd known how wonderful it would be to have grand-children, I'd have had them first.

SOURCE UNKNOWN

*L*et's bring back grand-mothers—the old-fashioned kind, who take you by the hand and lead you into the future, safe and savvy and smarter than your mother.

FLORENCE KING

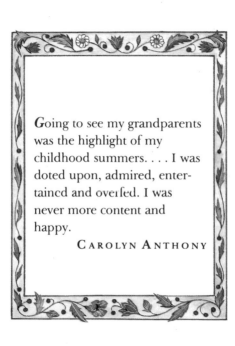

Going to see my grandparents was the highlight of my childhood summers. . . . I was doted upon, admired, entertained and overfed. I was never more content and happy.

CAROLYN ANTHONY

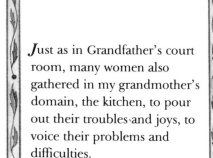

*J*ust as in Grandfather's court room, many women also gathered in my grandmother's domain, the kitchen, to pour out their troubles and joys, to voice their problems and difficulties.

ISAAC BASHEVIS SINGER

Grandmotherhood does not give us the right to speak without thinking, but only the right to think without speaking.

LOIS WYSE

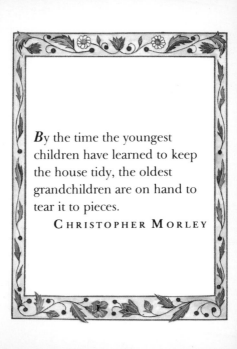

*B*y the time the youngest children have learned to keep the house tidy, the oldest grandchildren are on hand to tear it to pieces.

CHRISTOPHER MORLEY

Slow, Grandparents at play

*Sign in a Florida
mobile home park*

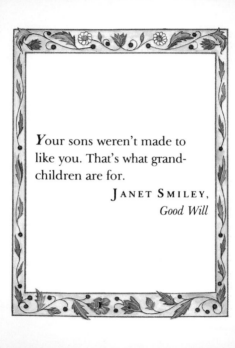

*Y*our sons weren't made to like you. That's what grand-children are for.

JANET SMILEY,
Good Will

*T*he threat of nuclear war and what it could do to my grandchildren's future was more than I could handle. I'll do this work until I can't anymore, or until God says, "Hey, that's enough—come home."

TRUDE BRITTON,
*member of
Grandmothers For Peace*

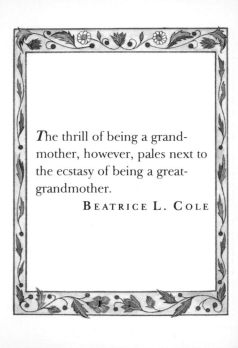

*T*he thrill of being a grandmother, however, pales next to
the ecstasy of being a great-
grandmother.

BEATRICE L. COLE

I was her little shadow, and that was just the way I wanted it. Goggy was two hundred years old and would let me chase her all around the big old house and tickle her. When I caught her, I didn't tickle her too hard because she could've broken.

CAROL BURNETT

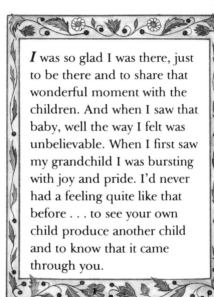

I was so glad I was there, just to be there and to share that wonderful moment with the children. And when I saw that baby, well the way I felt was unbelievable. When I first saw my grandchild I was bursting with joy and pride. I'd never had a feeling quite like that before . . . to see your own child produce another child and to know that it came through you.

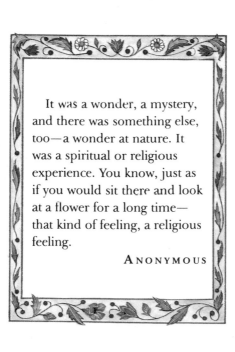

It was a wonder, a mystery, and there was something else, too—a wonder at nature. It was a spiritual or religious experience. You know, just as if you would sit there and look at a flower for a long time— that kind of feeling, a religious feeling.

ANONYMOUS

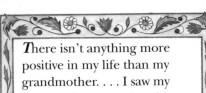

*T*here isn't anything more positive in my life than my grandmother. . . . I saw my mom and my grandmother go to work every day. I didn't know until I was an adult that there were different jobs for women and men. They never complained. To them, there was dignity in work. They were proud. Proud that they were never on welfare, and that they provided for their family.

GEORGETTE MOSBACHER

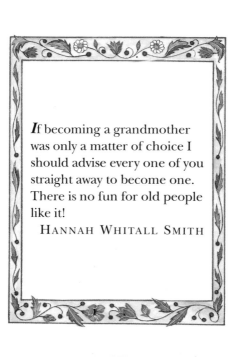

*I*f becoming a grandmother
was only a matter of choice I
should advise every one of you
straight away to become one.
There is no fun for old people
like it!

Hannah Whitall Smith

I loved my grandmother more than any other human being because she never lied, never told you what you wanted to hear, never compromised. She had a healthy hatred for all living human beings, all systems of government, all religion, except her own, of course, which was based on her intolerance of humanity with a little Judaism thrown in.

ROSEANNE BARR

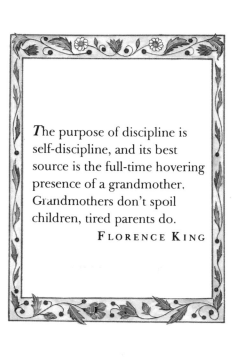

*T*he purpose of discipline is self-discipline, and its best source is the full-time hovering presence of a grandmother. Grandmothers don't spoil children, tired parents do.

FLORENCE KING

*H*er manner of storytelling evoked tenderness and mystery as she put her face close to mine and fixed me with her big, believing eyes. Thus was the strength that was developing in me directly infused from her.

MAXIM GORKY

*W*hat I learned from Grandma's stories was this: Women could do hard things and do them competently; problems could be worked out if you ignored what everyone else told you and did what the situation required; sometimes there are men around and sometimes not, but life goes on pretty much the same either way.

Sue Hubbell

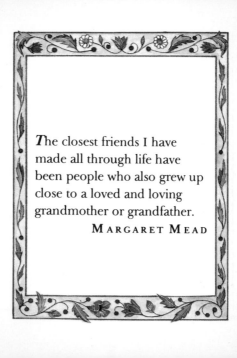

*T*he closest friends I have
made all through life have
been people who also grew up
close to a loved and loving
grandmother or grandfather.

MARGARET MEAD

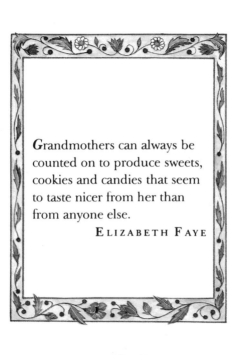

Grandmothers can always be counted on to produce sweets, cookies and candies that seem to taste nicer from her than from anyone else.

ELIZABETH FAYE

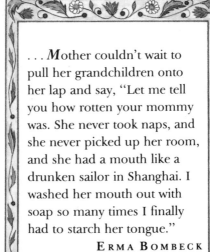

. . . *M*other couldn't wait to pull her grandchildren onto her lap and say, "Let me tell you how rotten your mommy was. She never took naps, and she never picked up her room, and she had a mouth like a drunken sailor in Shanghai. I washed her mouth out with soap so many times I finally had to starch her tongue."

ERMA BOMBECK

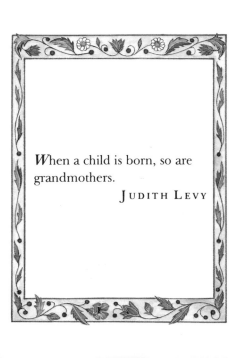

When a child is born, so are grandmothers.

JUDITH LEVY

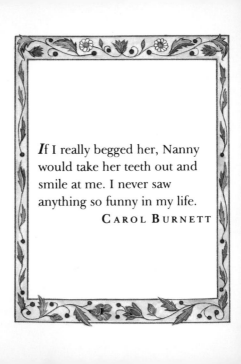

If I really begged her, Nanny
would take her teeth out and
smile at me. I never saw
anything so funny in my life.

CAROL BURNETT

[**G**randmother is someone] to cudel you when you have the mumphs.

[Grandmother is someone] to make you fat and then love you.

[Grandmother is someone] to spoil you and save you from your parents.

Grade school children's definitions,
What Is a Grandmother

Grandparents are always being told that they are living history to their grandchildren, that they give the children the reassurance of their roots. For me and many grandmothers I have talked to, it works the other way as well. They give *us* continuity.

RUTH GOODE

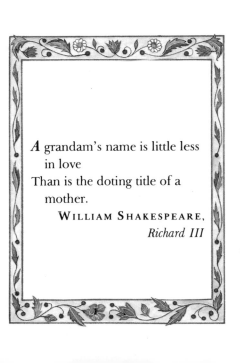

A grandam's name is little less
   in love
Than is the doting title of a
   mother.

WILLIAM SHAKESPEARE,
         Richard III

*M*y great-grandmama told my grandmama the part she lived through that my grandmama didn't live through and my grandmama told my mama what they both lived through and my mama told me what they all lived through and we were suppose to pass it down like that from generation to generation so we'd never forget.

GAYL JONES

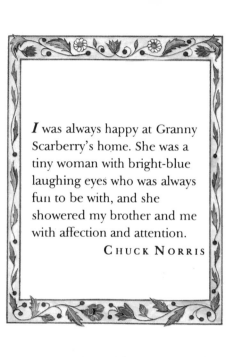

I was always happy at Granny Scarberry's home. She was a tiny woman with bright-blue laughing eyes who was always fun to be with, and she showered my brother and me with affection and attention.

CHUCK NORRIS

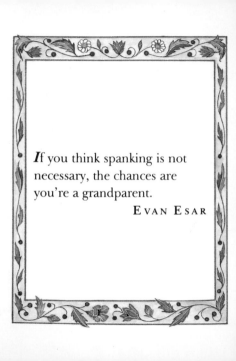

*I*f you think spanking is not
necessary, the chances are
you're a grandparent.

EVAN ESAR

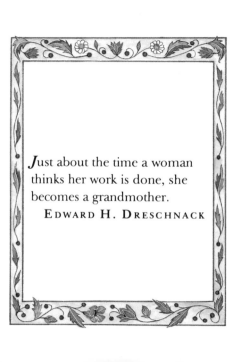

*J*ust about the time a woman
thinks her work is done, she
becomes a grandmother.

EDWARD H. DRESCHNACK

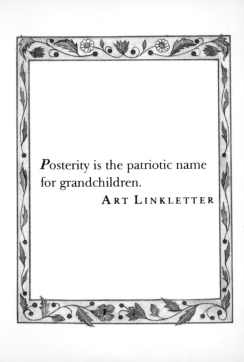

*P*osterity is the patriotic name
for grandchildren.

ART LINKLETTER

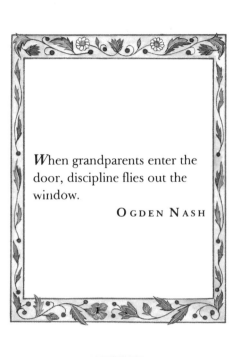

When grandparents enter the door, discipline flies out the window.

OGDEN NASH

*W*hile I was a child her great
affection for me, and her
intense care for my welfare,
made me love her and gave
me that feeling of safety that
children need.

BERTRAND RUSSELL,
on his grandmother

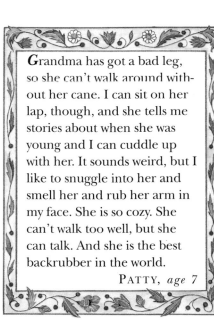

*G*randma has got a bad leg, so she can't walk around without her cane. I can sit on her lap, though, and she tells me stories about when she was young and I can cuddle up with her. It sounds weird, but I like to snuggle into her and smell her and rub her arm in my face. She is so cozy. She can't walk too well, but she can talk. And she is the best backrubber in the world.

PATTY, *age 7*

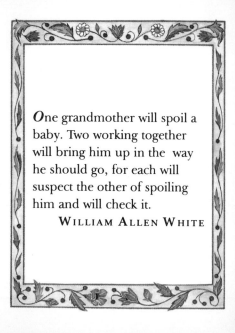

*O*ne grandmother will spoil a baby. Two working together will bring him up in the way he should go, for each will suspect the other of spoiling him and will check it.

WILLIAM ALLEN WHITE

*M*y grandmother made dying
her life's work.

HUGH LEONARD

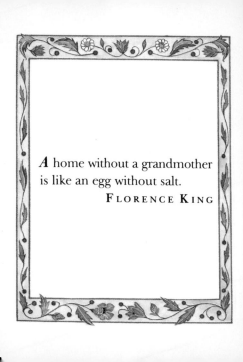

A home without a grandmother
is like an egg without salt.

FLORENCE KING

*T*he reason grandparents and grandchildren get along so well is that they have a common enemy.

SAM LEVENSON

*T*he first person ever to notice my music ability was not my father or my mother but Grandma Ada McGill back in Illinois. Grandma, who lived to be nearly a hundred, always remembered your name and recognized something about you, when somebody else might have needed a doggone scorecard to sort out all the children.

BARBARA MANDRELL

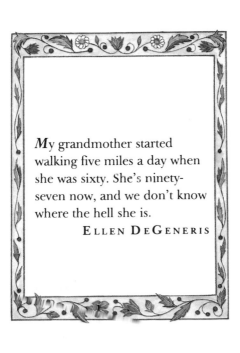

*M*y grandmother started walking five miles a day when she was sixty. She's ninety-seven now, and we don't know where the hell she is.

ELLEN DEGENERIS

God has a special place for
them in heaven and when
grandmother does eventually
go there she will be smiling
down, and on her lap will be
one of God's littlest angels—
the one that reminds her of
YOU.

ELIZABETH FAYE

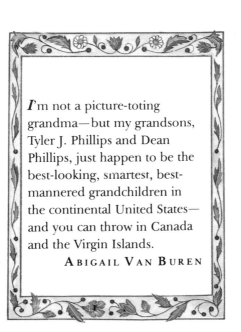

I'm not a picture-toting grandma—but my grandsons, Tyler J. Phillips and Dean Phillips, just happen to be the best-looking, smartest, best-mannered grandchildren in the continental United States—and you can throw in Canada and the Virgin Islands.

ABIGAIL VAN BUREN

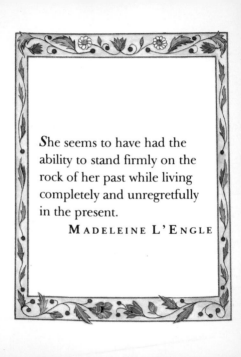

She seems to have had the
ability to stand firmly on the
rock of her past while living
completely and unregretfully
in the present.

MADELEINE L'ENGLE

*M*y grandmother is over eighty and still doesn't need glasses. Drinks right out of the bottle.

HENNY YOUNGMAN

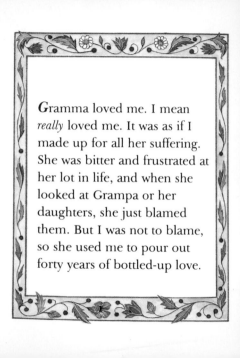

*G*ramma loved me. I mean *really* loved me. It was as if I made up for all her suffering. She was bitter and frustrated at her lot in life, and when she looked at Grampa or her daughters, she just blamed them. But I was not to blame, so she used me to pour out forty years of bottled-up love.

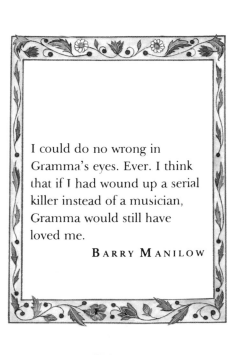

I could do no wrong in Gramma's eyes. Ever. I think that if I had wound up a serial killer instead of a musician, Gramma would still have loved me.

BARRY MANILOW

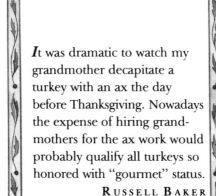

*I*t was dramatic to watch my grandmother decapitate a turkey with an ax the day before Thanksgiving. Nowadays the expense of hiring grandmothers for the ax work would probably qualify all turkeys so honored with "gourmet" status.

RUSSELL BAKER

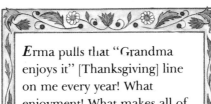

*E*rma pulls that "Grandma enjoys it" [Thanksgiving] line on me every year! What enjoyment! What makes all of them think a sixty-five-year old woman likes to get up at 4 A.M., arm-wrestle a naked turkey, stand over a toaster trying to make stale bread into fresh dressing, and spend ten hours making a meal that will take twelve minutes to inhale?

ERMA BOMBECK'S MOTHER

Grandma Gottfried never expressed much of a liking for anyone, but she appeared to have the least amount of ill will toward the Chihuahua.

DAVIDA ROSENBLUM

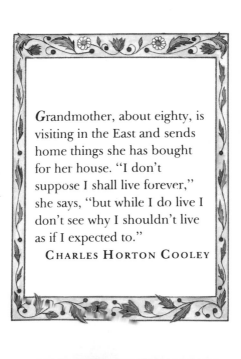

Grandmother, about eighty, is visiting in the East and sends home things she has bought for her house. "I don't suppose I shall live forever," she says, "but while I do live I don't see why I shouldn't live as if I expected to."

CHARLES HORTON COOLEY

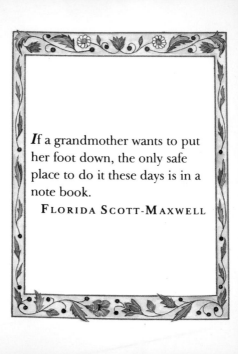

*I*f a grandmother wants to put
her foot down, the only safe
place to do it these days is in a
note book.

FLORIDA SCOTT-MAXWELL

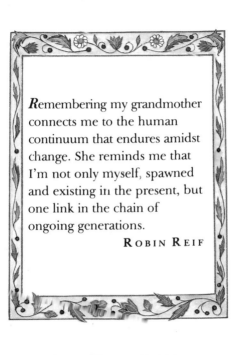

*R*emembering my grandmother connects me to the human continuum that endures amidst change. She reminds me that I'm not only myself, spawned and existing in the present, but one link in the chain of ongoing generations.

ROBIN REIF

I was an angel in her eyes, no matter what the facts were, no matter what anyone else happened to think.

JUDY LANGFORD CARTER

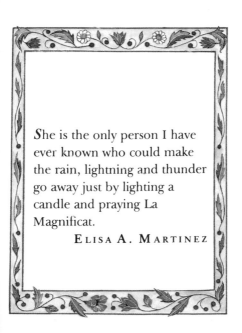

She is the only person I have ever known who could make the rain, lightning and thunder go away just by lighting a candle and praying La Magnificat.

ELISA A. MARTINEZ

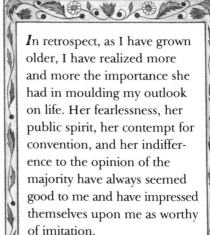

In retrospect, as I have grown older, I have realized more and more the importance she had in moulding my outlook on life. Her fearlessness, her public spirit, her contempt for convention, and her indifference to the opinion of the majority have always seemed good to me and have impressed themselves upon me as worthy of imitation.

BERTRAND RUSSELL

*T*here is a delight, a comfort, an easing of the burden, a renewal of joy in my own life, to feel the stream of life of which I am part going on like this.

BETTY FRIEDAN,
on being a grandmother

*B*ecoming a grandparent is a
second chance. For you have a
chance to put to use all the
things you learned the first
time around and may have
made mistakes on. It's all love
and no discipline. There's no
thorn in this rose.

DR. JOYCE BROTHERS

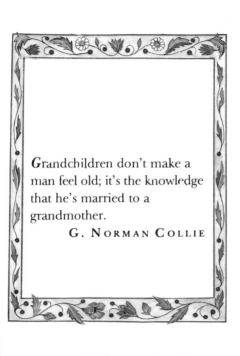

Grandchildren don't make a man feel old; it's the knowledge that he's married to a grandmother.

G. NORMAN COLLIE

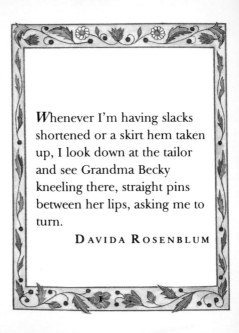

*W*henever I'm having slacks shortened or a skirt hem taken up, I look down at the tailor and see Grandma Becky kneeling there, straight pins between her lips, asking me to turn.

DAVIDA ROSENBLUM

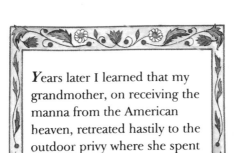

*Y*ears later I learned that my grandmother, on receiving the manna from the American heaven, retreated hastily to the outdoor privy where she spent the better part of the day restoring her intestinal equilibrium. The stomach is, perhaps, a more accurate emotional weather vane than even the heart.

BRENDA WEISBERG MECKLER

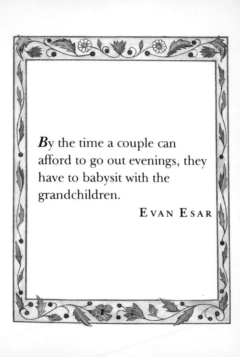

*B*y the time a couple can afford to go out evenings, they have to babysit with the grandchildren.

EVAN ESAR

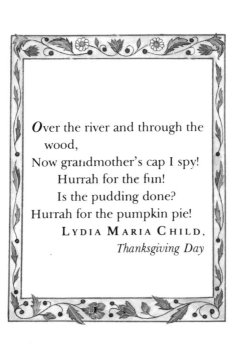

*O*ver the river and through the
  wood,
Now grandmother's cap I spy!
  Hurrah for the fun!
  Is the pudding done?
Hurrah for the pumpkin pie!

LYDIA MARIA CHILD,
  Thanksgiving Day

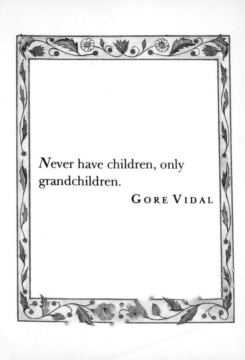

*N*ever have children, only grandchildren.

GORE VIDAL

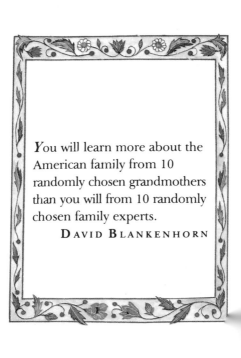

*Y*ou will learn more about the American family from 10 randomly chosen grandmothers than you will from 10 randomly chosen family experts.

DAVID BLANKENHORN

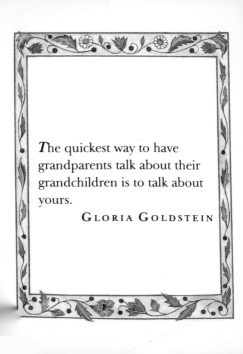

*T*he quickest way to have
grandparents talk about their
grandchildren is to talk about
yours.

GLORIA GOLDSTEIN

What in heaven's name is so strange about a grandmother dancing nude? I bet lots of grandmothers do it.

SALLY RAND

Whenever we had to visit Granny at Marlborough House, we always felt that we were going to be hauled over the coals for something we had done.

PRINCESS MARGARET

*N*anny never missed a night looking under the bed before she got in it. She said she wanted to make sure there wasn't a man under there. I always thought if there was, she'd scare him more than he'd scare her because she wore long underwear with a drop seat that sagged and her teeth were out.

CAROL BURNETT

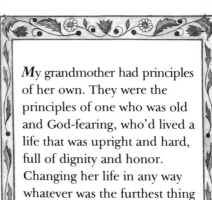

*M*y grandmother had principles of her own. They were the principles of one who was old and God-fearing, who'd lived a life that was upright and hard, full of dignity and honor. Changing her life in any way whatever was the furthest thing from her mind.

SVETLANA ALLILUYEVA,
Stalin's daughter

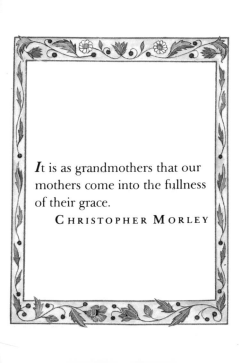

*I*t is as grandmothers that our mothers come into the fullness of their grace.

CHRISTOPHER MORLEY

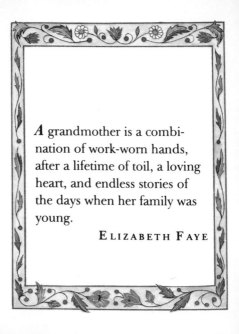

A grandmother is a combination of work-worn hands, after a lifetime of toil, a loving heart, and endless stories of the days when her family was young.

ELIZABETH FAYE

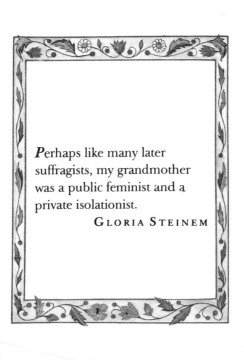

*P*erhaps like many later
suffragists, my grandmother
was a public feminist and a
private isolationist.

GLORIA STEINEM

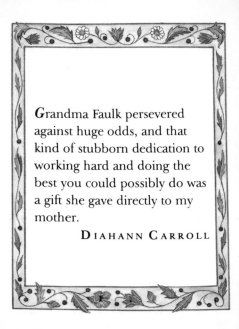

*G*randma Faulk persevered against huge odds, and that kind of stubborn dedication to working hard and doing the best you could possibly do was a gift she gave directly to my mother.

DIAHANN CARROLL

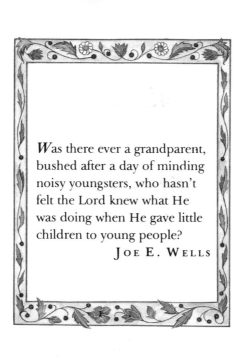

*W*as there ever a grandparent, bushed after a day of minding noisy youngsters, who hasn't felt the Lord knew what He was doing when He gave little children to young people?

JOE E. WELLS

*S*o many things we love are you, I can't seem to explain except by little things, but flowers and beautiful hand-made things — small stitches. So much of our . . . thinking— so many sweet customs and so much of our . . . religion. It is all *you*. I hadn't realized it before. This is so vague, but do you see a little, dear Grandma? I want to thank you.

ANNE MORROW LINDBERGH